MY MODEST BLINDNESS

Russell Brakefield

autofocus books
Orlando, Florida

Praise for *MY MODEST BLINDNESS*

"Out of a struggle with literary history, medical technology, and personal loss, Russell Brakefield gives us a prismatic, revelatory collection of poetry. We receive new angles from which to see what's right in front of us. We understand the visible world as one that becomes both more uncanny and more vibrant as it fades or is distorted. From what begins as great deprivation—this maker's vision—becomes the beginning of great wonder."
—**Mark Yakich**, author of *Poetry: A Survivor's Guide*

"There is something inescapably true in Russ Brakefield's second collection, *My Modest Blindness*. At the surface, it is an exploration of a writer's reckoning with ailment. A hybrid approach to capturing a fleeting visual landscape. A project that yields stunning observations of light, color and kinetic field. Perhaps in the spirit of field recording, as in his first collection, these poems make a journey through log and documentation. Along the way, Brakefield turns to old masters who navigated near or total blindness, such as Milton, Audre Lorde and importantly, Jorge Luis Borges. Amidst the beauty of these poems, there is a generosity in their frankness and disclosure. And beneath all that, there is the honesty the poems come to know: '…and what is living / but trying to find a sea bird inside a sea bird colored storm,' the poet writes. What a brave and haunting book."
—**francine j. harris**, author of *Here Is the Sweet Hand: Poems*

"Carrying both the ache of loss and the sensory-rich beauty of the blurred and non-visual worlds, *My Modest Blindness* is deep and transfixing. Beyond the book's apparent subject, Brakefield's poems serve as a side-door portrait of the human mind—its taunting fickleness, its sprawling web of memories and connections, the way it accepts while pushing against."
—**Joshua James Amberson**, author of *Staring Contest: Essays About Eyes*

"'What is belief but held breath,' asks Russell Brakefield in these vital poems of a disappearing self and 'learning to love different versions of shadow.' Too often we say 'to see' when we mean 'to know,' and I love how beautifully and playfully these poems blur the line between sight and knowledge, between knowledge and belief."
—**James Tate Hill**, author of *Blind Man's Bluff*

Published by Autofocus Books
PO Box 560002
Orlando, Fl 32856
autofocuslit.com

Poetry
ISBN: 978-1-957392-26-4

Cover Illustration ©Amy Wheaton
Library of Congress Control Number: 2023946214

MY MODEST BLINDNESS

Keratoconus, n. a slowly progressive abnormality in the cornea, which changes from its normal gradual curve to a more conical shape, causing distortion of vision.
—*Oxford Reference, Concise Medical Dictionary*

In the fullness of the years, like it or not,
a luminous mist surrounds me, unvarying,
that breaks things down into a single thing,
colorless, formless. Almost into a thought.
—**Jorge Luis Borges**

Table of Contents

I. Paper Boats

I will begin then says Borges   *by referring to my own modest blindness*

    a bindle unfurls behind him   images rolling off the lectern

and down aisles—   yellow tiger   grey wolfe in winter

    The color that shines in poetry   he says and wraps the yoke

of his years in linen   I'm wrapped in linen   my eyes are

    eyes like an emu's   an ostrich   and more surface

    always means   more surface to damage

In the examining room   Doc says *progressive* but means *degenerative*

     and I think of Homer   wine black waves like lashes

against the bow   Odysseus's terrible tears when the blind bard recounts

     Doc   in his white coat   carries storm clouds—

     my vision is a paper boat   drifting slowly out to sea

Even a feather's fake eye relays virility   royal blue blinks in the plume

proffers in the iris a waiting fortune   I swim between

image and abstraction   *What is dark within me, illumine*   says Milton

long after his darkness floods in   in the trees tonight

magpies pageant glossy tail pins   eyes turn in the sun   their story

held from me by disease and genetics   on the porch

I'm a cracked lens   a static soaked station   transistor broken

I'm a translator with no second language

What would you carry from a burning house?

      lovers   photographs   money   pets   I'm running

a survey   I'm taking a poll   I'm turning colors to stone

      to water   my notebooks swell with a catalogue

of delights of the visual world   in the moment just before it leaves me

     in the kitchen a crystal catches ultraviolet from the window

     and casts a band of brilliant blushes on the page—

Entry #7: In the garden a trio of purple heirloom tomatoes, their crowns ringed in neon green. A streak of dew hangs on each of their foreheads like sweat. The fine hair of their stems stands tall, pulsing with electricity of water, air, soil. A tag in the dirt tells me the varietal is Indigo Apple, though all year I've been calling them Bruises or Savory Plums or Skyline Just Before Nightfall.

Lit   the machine skips   a new alphabet swims the tiny box

       of his vision—   the boy version of me   tiny Es

turned like hieroglyphs   how to explain to him beginnings?

       how to warn him of that other blurry path

paradox of hindsight   double edged sword   etc.?

       even through gauze time allows you   every day

       to see sharper all that's come before

It begins for me as almost nothing   just a slow weeping at the edges

of frame   in the examining room a barn burns

inside the viewfinder   "I Only Have Eyes For You" on Muzak

cruel irony of fluorescent lighting   Doc says *Open wide*

press your palate to the plastic   topo maps come back scratched

with wobbly crop circles   Milosz says to be a poet you must behold

a map both distant and concrete   when I squint the world trickles

back to me   *Try not to squint*   says Doc and uses his hand

to describe a cornea bending to a boney crescent moon

Entry #12: Bright yellow lemons in a bowl on my mother's table. Steam on the cupboards and her pearl blue eyes. The kitchen curtains' perfect hand stitch.

Slacked   the cornea slips to a new shape   parenthetical

        genetic misstep and I'm spirited away behind a wall of water

streetlights wander drunk at twilight   *One eye almost always swerves*

        before the other   they tell me   and so goes the right side

my dominant hand missing a shake   my leading shoulder baffled

        by doorframes   by her embrace   what a simple pleasure

to always know where you are in relation to the other

        objects in the world   where's the edge of the lake and where

the edge of the body?   who's to say the fires burning in the fields

        aren't just delicate pink lanterns riding on the wind?

Then seeing and vision are two rivers broke apart

some faces I can see when far away and when close up

folds behind the eyes holding tight the façade   Borges: *Thank God*

for slow nightfall   but in the park today I flail my arms

like a frightened bird   a crane   a heron   I beckon at

a copse of spindly box elder trees   in the shade below

is a face I know that is suddenly a face I've never seen before

Entry #13: My father's hands creasing a broadleaf in the yard to show me the glow of a near ripe melon. Pink meat, cantaloupe glistening like stardust. Fresh grass and a little rust from the fishing knife he used to open the rind and cut the flesh. His sun-toned palms push away seeds and carve a smile-shaped gash of moon.

One in two thousand will experience some form of mild to severe

bulging

coning   thinning   blur

sensitivity   cloud   corona   glare

rigid   gas permeable   transplant   cane

In traffic my windshield splinters   my vision and light rain

     casting me behind an opaque shade   at the stoplight

a man singing outside the liquor store is me   or my shadow

     streaky mirrors snap in the trees   a monk's bronze collar

around the sky   the light before winter is winter   untying

     the phone lines   a pair of ghosts step from their tennies

I could raze the earth on these visions   or I could find nothing

     but madness   revisions dance at the corners of my eyes—

a lost pasture   another life altogether   my ghost body

     wandering the peripheries   flickering

Entry #19: A white boat sliding back and forth across the deepest lake I know. Like in the Gilbert poem, it carries part of me away each day. I watch myself disappear through a grove of aspens. Bark wrapped like reams of paper, the future scratched in their trunks in dirty cursive, an already unintelligible script.

II. PATHOLOGY

I try to work out the rods and cones   molecular geometry

     of my new reality   a string on my finger to remember

the other end dropped through the ether and tied

     to a different version of myself—   a man who can see

a mote ply a needle's ring and write it into a perfect sonnet

     who can gather dust in handsome iambs on the head of a pin

In a normal specimen   the retina waits like a blank page

      at the back of the eye   light taps like a quill and turns

to electrical signal   then a relay race inside the brain   the baton

      of the visual world passed on and on and on until

it lands in the corridor that gives shape and contour   the room

      that parts clouds or spots a single golden poppy shouting

from the trash and pokeweed on the roadside   that draws

      moonlight in thin blue bars across a naked shoulder

Entry #24: Moon broke in half. One half on the sidewalk, the other in the clouds. Two half-moons bright enough to see her on the porch. The shadows on her face as she turns away to smile— otherworldly angles cut above her mouth. The arc of her back as she leans down to paint the cosmos on her toenails.

At the cliff's edge   bad air erases the valley's makeup   high school couples

and photogs stalk the viewing stave   flank the fence

that holds us on our perch—   sightseers   leaf peepers   minor cosmonauts

a Katy Perry playlist on a too loud boombox   I squint

and forms clip into my vantage—   mountain   fence line

jackpine   a sense of being closer to the living

relaxed and I'm back again to clouded canvas   black dog beside me

lifts his nose to read the news   what does he see here

that I miss?   maybe not much   maybe only an itch in the cortex

or maybe a million small truths held just out of reach

Entry #30: At dusk, fresh sparks of graffiti lighting up the train bridge. A purple crown breaks cement below the trestle. On the river's bank, a boy holds a fish in his hand, or a boy holds an oil slick, or a boy holds a squirming bag of rainbow coins.

Evenings I watch sun cut blurry rainbows through the kitchen window

what I've said before as curse I say now as consecration

I say it to the dishwater   I say it to the charming

last light of summer   Borges: *At nightfall*

the things closest to us seem to move away

from our eyes   the visible world has moved away from my eyes

perhaps forever

I hide my large print on the nightstand   now that I know **bold**

means italics   I know that **bold** means   usually

someone screaming inside their own head   **I'm screaming inside**

my own head tonight   everything I've done and said today

printed in **bold** as soon as I lie down   and in selfie mode I've noticed

a stuck smile line   and **I'm not sure I've smiled enough**

to have earned it   the average person smiles fifty times a day

says the search engine   children **still** caged at the border

still murdered in their tiny school chairs   **hospitals flooding**

deserts on fire   a reddit thread "How to die with a smile

on your face"   gives advice that is both physical and abstract:

Never do bad things. Never think bad of others. Avoid vanity.

Avoid direct sunlight.   **I cover the cover** of my large print novel

frivolous and mass market and murdery

we are all paragraphs sliding slowly off the page

Some gospels held that Mary and the apostles could not see

the savior's face on the road or on the shoreline

their boats bobbing out of reach of the risen   is progress to healing

what seeing is to salvation?   on the news today

even the lifeless excel at vision   machines whir and click and sputter

recognizing the intimate   delicate patterns of human expression

Entry #32: Campus chapel at dusk. Organ pipes like massive, golden lungs. In the front pew, rapt and oblivious, a boy or a small man weeps violently into his sweater. The sun flits through the stained glass and illuminates scraps of lifted dust like miracles or like a swarm of angry wasps.

A partial list of animals that can recognize human faces—

        pigs   sheep and pigeons   cows

        most domestic pets   the wasp   the crow

        the honeybee   some fish even   a dozen

        other insects and invertebrates

faces go first for me   after landscapes and posted signage

      so the order is   global   local   personal   essential

a telescope of loss   but I like that I remember dead people

      as their younger selves   and I'll begin to remember the living

that way too   and that these days auras on streetlamps hang

      like glowing halos   moonlets   planetary rings

      the lit crowns of early Renaissance paintings

Entry #38: Late night, the house across the street winks. One lit window and one pulled shade. A grey paw reaches from the storm drain like the glove of some tiny, hungry magician. A mime or clown. A bank robber casing the gutter. In the inky pool below the curb swim his two deep-set, glowing eyes. He only need blink them to disappear.

I fill journals too with notes on sightless animals—

       moles and crickets   the huntsman spider

       and deep-sea lobsters   flatworms   catfish

       snakes and lizards

on Amazon I buy the Richard Burton *Equus* but can't bring myself

       to watch   all this research feels masochistic—

keeping catalogue   blinding horses   you only live once in one body

       and adaptation is eons in the making   I turn on a rerun

of *Seinfeld* and George is spotting dimes without his glasses

       I'm sick with this coincidence   or how obsession turns

the world into a world of coincidence   I'm sick of pathologizing

       basic cable   outside the bats have begun to drop in swooping arcs

above the streetlamps—   a pilot for a television show that is deep darkness

       I hear them feasting   I feel their sightless dance

For the blind   Borges says   darkness is a gradient

   the color black also twisted   to a

greenish or bluish mist   I'm learning to hold distinction

   like the very best memory

of a lover who skipped town and didn't leave a note

   learning to love different versions of shadow

my left eye (a wingtip needing polish)

   and my right (a coal truck tipped over on the pass)

Entry #45: Piano keys along the ceiling. Interval of dark, short bar of light. Every home I've lived in reliant on traffic for its somnolent dance steps. The morning slopes in and sings, bar by bar, its ancient insomniac song.

III. A BRIEF HISTORY OF CORRECTIVE TECHNOLOGY

The first lens was born for language   by a bead of convex glass

      Catullus reads Petrarch   by a bead of convex glass

Catullus lets Homer swim laps and invents the avant-garde

     below my own loupe today I open to a sonnet   that whirring

square machine   and thank the old masters for the way

     this simple box tells me   no matter the blur   how to read

where to turn   how about form for a refuge?   how about pattern

     meter?   line?   how about repetition?   how about a boat

passing back and forth on the same lake each day?   a boat that looks to me

     like a tight quatrain pulled through the current

     by a nearly invisible string

- <>   How does the eye work?
- <>   How does the eye see?
- <>   How does the eye see color?
- <>   Who said the eye is the window to the soul?
- <>   Is the soul knowable?
- <>   Is the soul visible to those who know it?
- <>   How does the eye protect itself?
- <>   What do they use to cut into a cornea?
- <>   Where does an image start?
- <>   How is a laser different from a scalpel?
- <>   How does the eye work with the brain?
- <>   Where does language go in the dark?

Doc says *there are options*   taps his pen   *but only when things get really bad*

and the body   like a poem   becomes elusive   turns fluid

Hard contacts   he says   *a gel in test trials*   worse case is a dead man's

eyes swapped for mine on the table   I'm picturing

Clockwork Orange   Cyclops   Levar Burton   I'm picturing

a life of seeing through a stranger's lens   *Poetry lifts the veil*

from the hidden beauty of the world   said Shelly but did not mean it

in terms of invasive surgery   I've been googling

the word *augment*   taking podcasts like probiotics   one on prosthetics

one on robotics   an oral history of the first corrective lens

tells me frames were built first of teeth and fur and animal bone

even then making someone whole

meant making them less human

Entry #51: Traffic swerved to part the herd, elk down to root the still soft earth near the highway. Snow-laced hay. Fields of low fog. Taillights burning. In the median, a dozen furry, lurching backs. Then they shrink to flecks in the rearview, breath lifting like thought clouds above them. My own breath invisible, barely there at all.

Early lenses were forged on a hearth   flames licking glass

                 into the desired thickness   like in other parts of history

the rich and the ingenious find the clearest vantage   innovation born

                 of necessity but also privilege—   Galileo's mortar and pestle

and then   Martin's margins   a fancy pair of over ears

                 pocket glasses   prinze nez   spectacles shaped like scissors

not much can help the damaged loupes I look through   not money

                 not science   technology's tideline leading

forward and back   not the waiting room's choppy waters

                 not the doctors' circling fins

Entry #54: Passenger train ringing River North, a brow of mauve mountains up above. Cranes holding up nothing but progress, the promise of progress. The promise of commerce and erasure. Plastic coated buildings. Rooftop bars. Smoke screens. At dusk, the city nods off, its flues sending up plumes like a hundred tired sighs.

The brain is a camera   the eye a lens   the world is a camera

      the brain a lens   Sontag: *Bleak factory buildings*

and billboard-cluttered avenues look as beautiful through the camera's eye

      as churches and pastoral landscapes

the moss-covered post office at the end of the street   blurs

      a beautiful   crumbling monument   the brain is

      a camera   the eye a lens   busted camera   shattered lens

On a postcard above my desk   a series of frescoes

    by Tommaso da Modena—   one cardinal dons a pair

of silver spectacles and one sports a single suspended lens

    and both bend over their work like small gods straining

to see the worlds they've made   in the mirror

    of my computer screen   I lean in to see the world I've made

a world of brilliant images   a world in black and white

    the text brings me back from the sightless life

    the text walks like spiders in the rain

Entry #55: Sunset over the valley—light passing through bad air and torching the abundance of particles there. Fires somewhere far away singing their colorful songs. So crimson it consumes everything. This, at least, I can see. Or I see the unseeable that is made filmic. A shade of red so strange it lances even my rotten, thinning lens. A shade of red so red I won't be able to render it.

Surrounded by systems to check us   I'm tasked too

      with fooling the machines   with finding ways to live

at the DMV I close one eye and squint   I hold my phone close

      when no one's looking   I sit up front at lectures and walk

the rooms I teach   trying to snatch faces from a shadowy crowd

      and embed them   I turn to audiobooks   ambient records

birdsong   I learn directions by color   by graffiti and murals

      on the corner   distinct designs   a twisted tree

in the neighborhood or a specific patch of pinyon telling me to turn left

      up the old jeep road   a dozen other hazards hang just out of focus

unwelcome detours   machines I won't be able to chump   and what

      will change when they read this   when I can no longer pretend

      I'm not slipping under   not wandering into mist

What would you recommend?   I ask the waiter

    and he looks at me like he knows   I can't see

beyond the tea light on the table   an insect climbs across

    the wine list like more crawling text   I take down

my lenses   *Chianti?*   he says   guessing I'm a philistine

    and not going blind   not terrified   *petit verdot*

she says   and leans across the table to touch me

    her hand is a cup of small affection balanced

on my knee   a cup of pity too   two glasses

    appear on the table   full of something thin and bloody

Entry #57: At city center, the corner of a parking garage dappled with color. Blood red and cobalt, cerulean and admiral. Waves of a mural climb the building, summoning abstract clouds and mountains, dreamscape shapes in primary color. Are those eyelashes or antlers framing the garage? An eyeball or a river dripping near the edge? A vibrant puzzle made for better eyes. A perfect mystery all the same.

Reading *Labyrinths* on the night bus by the intermittent desk lamp

of STOP REQUESTED signs   my eyes wear felt

sing like spades in a midnight garden   I heard once

when the first lamps were lit   people cowered in the streets

shame suddenly a living thing   the devil given extra legs

I know my own hellhounds even here in the shadows

at my stop nothing but a denim sky   the lamp I left burning

in the window   guilt   regret   and the crunch of snow

like rodents chewing dusk beneath my feet

Entry #59: City skyscape at midnight. All the neon signage built to keep us in the grids. The fluorescent net of traffic like its own respiratory system. Then, on the outskirts, a single pair of taillights dips into the fog of a low hill, and I imagine two men carrying torches. Two men, maybe brothers, echoing second shift, singing together as they walk the long road home together.

IV. ANCESTORS

But darkness is   the scientists say   a prepared fear

        and darkness is   the historians say   karma

atonement   eye for an eye   we answer for our ancestors

        for the marauders in our ancestors' midst   the curtain

falls and catches a tripwire in the body   our muscles constrict

        our organs dilate   even the eyes pelt and wait

for scratch or bite   I turn to music and language   to the music

        of language   for each loss   a song   I measure

my days in metronomes   I hear his voice even after the lectures end:

        You must replace the visual world with something else

Entry #60: Above the amphitheater, a string of beaming beads. A carpet of fireflies. A rope of glowing teeth. My body swells with music, synesthesia of the city lights, rocks catching sound like a basket and passing it back. Somewhere in the darkness behind me, I imagine mule deer skuttling on the slick rock. I can almost see them, their fur draped like loose cloaks. I watch them walk the hills like echoes.

The radio host says ducks sleep with one eye popped—

     protection mechanism   a glassy shield to watch

for snake or crow or hawk   all the talons threaded to strike

     so then   I think   one eye's not so bad

in college I read poem after poem by mid-century imagists

     with vision problems   Creeley   Harrison

clipped bricks of text about the wounded male psyche

     essays where men were always winking and slobbering

like pop-eyed pugs   my own right eye is a headlight tonight

     frozen over   the brighter beam cut off   I've left

my browser up to a Ted Talk about self-deception   how we mis-see

     ourselves   I'm at home alone again   in the laptops glow

my reflection enters stage left   then disappears

     when the camera pans out   fade to back   cue applause

Entry #61: In the foothills at dawn, a herd of horned sheep hiding on the hillside. Scrubby, beige coats. This is a camouflage for all of us. When they turn their crowns, they turn from stone. When they turn their crowns, they turn to fur and blood and bone. Such is the steady shine of biology. Their persistence. Their adaptation. And us just clumsy predators, stalking, oblivious, into the past.

Must have read Audre Lorde every day in my twenties

the way I said I did to women to seem open and like I knew

what I was doing with my body   I'm trying to work out

if what the kids call simping is shot through with the same

deceptions   how much of being young is lying to yourself

about lying to others?   in the stacks tonight I want to puke

up the years I lost looking for books   finding them

and never cracking them open   in an interview

in a critical essay in a literary journal on the internet   Lorde writes

I was born almost blind   I have an image of imaging all the time

my hands are shaking   I have an image of imaging all the time

a bare tree wears black leaves in the quad below   a clock

of black birds mis-set for the season   black birds rubbing shoulders

like leaves   snow like a fogged mirror on the ground below

Entry #62: Her bright dress the color of clouded sunlight. Her skin the color of baked stone. Her blue eyes the color, tonight, of wind.

In myth sight is taken for being monster and taken for taking sight

      taken to punish   to decapitate   to avenge   to humiliate

taken for making mistakes   exchanged for musical tongue   or longer life

      taken for sleeping with your mother   or taken for

offenses against the gods   I scour the internet tonight for better insights—

      WebMD   drugs.com   Guess what Ashley Olsen looks like now?

I can reframe any ailment as punishment with proper encouragement

      remember pushing your brother from the swing set

when you were nine?   remember watching *Field of Dreams*

      after she told you her father had died and then just leaving?

just going back to your apartment to drink alone?   the message boards

      are always either quiet or ripe with the expected nonsense—

conspiracies   witchcraft   eye for an eye old testament smitings

      all of us searching for a savior or a point of origin   all of us burning

      faceless effigies   walking lost in a wake of smoke

Every branch decades back broken down by smoke

my grandad dead at sixty-one   his wife later   blue dye

to mark the cellular mutations   the other side too   losing leaves

in the mist   even my mother   lungs clean forty years

still dreams of drawing a filter   on *Madmen* Don lights up

and I feel the neural hitch   itchy pull to the parking lot

on *Madmen* Betty lights up in her nightgown and I squirm

only when my vision started to slip that I thought to quit

on *Madmen*   Burt Cooper lights up   and I think he looks like me

or like I might look when I'm old   should I make it there intact

only when my vision blurred did I think about what it meant

only when the old poet read to us in class from "The Nightingale"

and blindfolded our eyes and made us sniff tins of cumin   tobacco

pepper   rose hips   his voice billowing

I cannot see what flowers are at my feet

nor what soft incense hangs up in the boughs

Entry #63: A charred larch grove lurking in lined stanzas behind the river. An ancient poem. The stumps wear green crowns, shoots of rebirth adorning their brows. Beyond that the forest is alive and healthy or the forest is burnt and dead. What is belief but held breath? A fire going out and then waiting for another to catch.

Frida and Diego at the DAM and I am   per usual

    standing too close to the tombstone   *Self Portrait with Monkeys*—

bird of paradise erupting over her right shoulder is my favorite part

    one ochre leaf like a slice of ripe fruit   the docents circle

like somber wolves   they stalk and whisper *please back up*

    oil on masonite   I may never see this painting again

in my life   I want to tell them   but move on instead

    to the murals in the other room—   counterfeits

simulacra   backlit and printed on massive canvas—

    where I can lean in so close

    I'm practically made of brushstrokes

Entry #71: The orange-red stain on Frida's lips. Her cheeks. The delicate petals haunting her shoulder. Lime green veins interrupting the leaves. The silver tip of each primate's nose, each ear. Four sets of animal eyes—wet and watching— that follow me through the gallery like the eyes of four shaggy, steadfast angels.

My mother's mother's eyes wrecked by thick webs at the end

    of her life   her mind too wrapped in a Styrofoam film

time like milk poured over a life lived   my father's mother too

    feeling through a sheet of fog   we joked about her smoking

dope   one more script   one radical turn in her final months

    maybe all this is a way to say I don't want to live

the symptoms of the end of a life in its middle   here   see my cowardice

    my attachment   my vanity   *Simply one of the styles of living*

says Borges   and   *Happiness is its own end*   he leaves a trail

    of mantras   wells I dig with a reluctant trowel

scrolls I struggle to unroll   songs sung by birds I can't identify

    long gone birds   gone extinct   birds alive only in my dreams

Entry #75: Technicolor fingers of larkspur. Mallow and mariposa lilies. A hillside smeared in mule ears, blooming pads of butter. My mother and father move on the path in front of me like quaking aspens. At this distance, their branches tell the best story. Across the valley, beyond the river, cattle drive like another river. An oxbow of brown and white haunches. Nose rings flitting like little silver fish. Occasional antlers float the surface like downed logs caught in current.

V. IN BETWEEN WORLDS

Borges found the death of one sense an open door to others:

    I have lost the visible world   to reclaim another

I walk the lake today snubbing the molted shoreline opposite me

    furry ripple by the dock   indistinct cormament

shrouded   insignificant feathers   a stubborn wordcloud

    nags the back of my neck   asks for details I cannot reach

but I suppose all writing is an attempt to capture a precise image

    with an imprecise instrument   and what is living

    but trying to find a sea bird inside a sea bird colored storm

And then in the yard   two fat sparrows or two lithe wrens

    or two gloves left out and pummeled by rain

or two severed hands   fingers still moving to count

    syllables   counting syllables   counting syllables

on the severed fingers of the severed hand   left out in the garden

    or none of that   just a foxglove on the fence line

    opening its palm   fanning its battered petals

On my thirty-fifth birthday I roam alone the field of my body

      I part tall lupines and dew-soaked verbena   I fall into the guts

of a fog-soaked valley   count a rosary of polished stones

      beneath the river   it took a pandemic for me to see

I'm not alone inside my afflictions   even here   just river and cloud

      and a single magpie bruising the lodgepole   we're all looking

for a clear window   all hunting a still pool   *All day,*

      all night, the body intervenes   says Woolf *The creature within*

can only gaze through the pane   the body lacks plot   she says elsewhere

      but here is a story of the body—   I do not walk into the river

I do not slip beneath the moving water   I do not   do not

      I do not   let the current drag me under

Entry #78: On the trail a row of common mullein dotted with golden pollen. The stalks wave in unison like lit candles, like a row of faint flames.

Harvest the blur   step into a life of shadow   I let myself

    be led like I'm saddled to a broke colt   a broke colt

that leads me on instinct to the most beautiful mistakes

    in the pasture   this is literal   this is metaphor

I narrow my eyes like a hawk on the fence line   I smell chicory

    turn an ear   the ringing bells of far-off water

I take off my gloves   to feel the air   her hot coat

    like sunset in my fingers   this is literal   this is metaphor

    here in the shadows   I see everything at once

Entry #84: Rusted Cadillac wrecked below the cliffside, just a Coke can crumpled in the trees. A scarf dropped on the path that turns to a rotting crow. A coiled snake on the trail that turns as fast to a skuttling, fallen leaf. The too fat carpenter moth beating at my brow that for a moment is a crescent moon descended to kiss my forehead.

The poem emerges on the page the same as a street sign

    or a high hanging menu at a lunch counter   closed captioning

in the theater   which is to say given to me by someone else

    which is to say there is immense pleasure

in an idea falling into focus slowly   bit by bit

    think of searching the walls of a dark room for a switch

but think too of feeling that switch suddenly beneath your finger

    and the wash of light after and the room illuminated

making something new out of darkness   something alive

    and singular   how it is as you imagined and also not

    and what beauty and truth alight in that moment

My catalogue reads like a bed of shells dragged and dragged

on a steady current   no matter the jagged edges   no matter

fractures or barbs   abundance grinds everything back

to a soft and luminous dust   I collect pattern and pigment

and movement like a man married to his moth board   I snapshot

skin and landscape   detail sunrise and green green grass

and rainfall pooling in a shallow puddle   a byproduct of my vanishing

vision is looking with a desperate eye   here is the other world

Borges spoke about and that world   I know now   is gratitude

mountains ground to sand and sifted through my greedy fingers

eons of image   like gravel in my hands

Entry #89: Rudbeckias behind the bakery. Butter-yellow bunches break open the sidewalk. A bear claw breeze. A gust of French roast and exhaust from the city bus. Mountains in the distance wear a confectionary crown, sweet reminder of our geologic pasts. Across the street, neon leaves of the dispensary sign spark on, memento of our modern oblivions.

What is it I'm trying to say here?   that like Borges

      this fog will make me see?   that a poet must distort

distort   distort?   that all infirmities are   at last

      inevitable?   a mere byproduct of being alive?   is it enough

that my metaphors grow stranger each day?   that my ear curls

      in a new horn   tighter   newly attune to pitch and turn?

is strange beauty a good trade for losing the faces of the ones I love?

      in this life   I know   there is no one to one

I'm working my way out from under this like a writer does

      which is to say from inside a glass box

where the glass is one day veined like quartz

      where the glass is one day streaked with blood

Maybe here's the lesson   foaming up from this pitch-plum sea

    humility   and after that   even more humility

everyday   I know less and less   and thank god

        there's my hand in front of my eyes   it's a witch's claw

a hoof or talon   a monkey's paw   no hand at all

        elegant fingers   crooked bones   darkness

where a hand once was   and beyond is all   I cannot

        see   beyond is all I cannot   hold or write

or fully imagine   or signify   thank god

        for what I know now   I may not ever know

Entry #91: October, last call, all the bees still sweating on the clovers. Past the abandoned water tower, hooves cloven along the fire road, blue-brown river winched against the sky. Even a paper coffee cup, glorious too today, wedged against a flaming patch of desert sumac. A scar for sure, but also a reminder someone else was here.

I am ashamed to have spoken of my own personal case

      says Borges   *except that people always hope for confessions*

and who am I to deny them   and so me too   I open up

      my eyes for you to look inside   I have yet to find

my way into complete shadow   I have yet to see

      completely   the fortunate music this fog

affords me   the visible world is a line break   a minor chord

      a painting with hearts and thorns   from the yard tonight

I watch grey-green tracers fill the sky   echo of downtown fireworks

      or perhaps a window into the past   or a window to the future

my soul returning as a willow or halo of flame

      back to the infinite winds of the universe

Entry #93: High desert. Rocks soaked in neon lichen. Neon lichen breathing, then breathing again for all of us. Undergrowth blushed by orange Artist Paintbrush. History's visible texts—stripped shale, raptor track, bone bed. screaming hawk. The bowl below is a scraped ocean. A diary of death and resurrection. I squint and capture it today inside my little notebook. I write it down and cut time open.

VI. CODA

A writer   Borges says   *must believe*

     whatever happens to him is an instrument

       everything has been given for an end

Entry #94: A stack of images—tight cursive on the back of a napkin— like small waves on a white sea. Somewhere inside, a poem about love or loss or about my mother's hands. Somewhere inside, a truth I've not yet seen.

Entry #96: A marble dropped in a glass teacup. Purple cat's eye shades the margins of this page.

Entry #97: A dozen fires burning in the shade of the barn today, a dozen orange thimbles trembling in the purple sage beside the garden. Each bee like a molecule or a tiny planet in the milky brush. And from the porch, it is one mauve breath, a struck snare, solar notes bending back to the earth.

Entry #100: A small line above her left eye I've never noticed because I've never looked, or because I've never needed to look this hard before.

    Blindness is not a misfortune   Borges says

       right before the lecture ends   *it is one more instrument*

  among many   and so I take up my pen

      or some new instrument even—

   let there always be something new—

      and begin   again   to play

NOTES AND ACKNOWLEDGEMENTS

Unless otherwise noted, the italicized material in this book comes from Jorge Luis Borges's lecture "On Blindness," delivered in Buenos Aires on August 3, 1977.

A version of "Entry #13" first appeared in the chapbook *Our Natural Satellite*, published by Harvard Square Press.

***

A great deal of gratitude is owed to Keith Taylor, who encouraged me to write about this experience in the first place, then took me out for a beer to ask me how I was doing. Thanks Keith for your guidance and for your friendship.

Thanks to my dramaturgy brothers Aaron Burch and Matthew Kirkpatrick, my first readers for just about everything. Thanks for keeping me writing and laughing. Thanks for believing in this project even before I did.

Thanks to Jeffrey Pethybridge, Anne Waldman, and the Naropa Summer Writing Program for supporting my work and for giving me a stage on which to first read these poems.

To Michael and the Autofocus team, thank you for your enthusiasm for this project, and for your hard work bringing this book to life.

Thanks to my family for their love and encouragement, specifically to my mother, who got me my first pair of glasses and turned on the leaves in the trees.

Thanks to Joe Horton, who always reads the scoreboard for me when I can't.

And to Aubrey, my best friend and my love—thanks for driving me home in the dark.

ABOUT THE AUTHOR

Russell Brakefield is the author of *Field Recordings* (Wayne State University Press). His writing has appeared in the *Indiana Review, New Orleans Review, The Common, Rattle,* and elsewhere. He is a graduate of the University of Michigan's Helen Zell Writers' Program, and he has been awarded fellowships from the University of Michigan Musical Society, the Vermont Studio Center, and the National Parks Service. He is assistant professor in the University Writing Program at the University of Denver.

ⓐ

Printed in the USA
CPSIA information can be obtained
at www.ICGtesting.com
CBHW021920260124
3769CB00024B/596